Table of Contents

Everyone in the world needs something! That thing may be a serious tangible thing like a car, a house, a wife, or children, or a non-tangible thing like a prayer, happiness, pleasure, longer life, respect, and a job. After listing these too many wishes with nothing in common at all, I think it is time to create a link between them.

Many people go to pray to get a job so that they can buy a house, buy a car, and get wives so that they can get kids, and then be happy while also getting the pleasure that comes with that happiness, and in that whole process getting longer lives and respect.

Now, let's try to make all those life's wishes clearer and more straightforward, to get to the point of what we are going to talk about! To be more simplistic, the denominator of our worldly wishes is money (writing the book, I tried to highlight it, but I didn't want to spoil the surprise).
Money is simply what everybody wants. We don't want those useless papers but the value associated with them. Quoting Yuval Noah Harari in Homo Sapiens, "Everybody wants money because everybody else wants money". Therefore, this book is built on the simple fact that money is what everybody wants, without considering a few uncertainties. Thus, we live hoping that getting the money is the only major problem we have, and getting plenty of it will solve everything else, which is quite true. It turns out that getting money is a big problem on its own which needs much attention.

It is so hard to take a block of cheese from a mouse, knowing that the same mouse wants that cheese, as it is to take money from people who want that money so bad like you. And this is where the problem arises, as to how people can make money from people who want it on nearly the same level.
And here comes the moneymaking system! Do you remember those needs I listed above? Well, we want them too, but apart from money, they have little or no relation at all among themselves!

A pro tip, whenever you see a loophole or glitch in the matrix, try to extract it in your favor as much as you can, if you don't harm other people in the process. Luckily, those needs, have a loophole that we can extract.

But before I talk about that loophole, let me tell you a story associated with it.

Once upon a time, there were two powerful kingdoms on a Planet called Kurya, one kingdom was called Rima, and the other was called Ruma. Rima lived north of the border valley called Koma, while Ruma lived south of Koma. In other words, Rima was north of Ruma but far apart, being separated by a very huge and dry valley called Koma.

For most of their history, the two kingdoms were involved in constant and bloody wars which claimed many lives of people on both sides. In case of wars, the two kingdoms with their huge armies would clash in the Koma. The two Kingdoms' wars would last for days, and rarely for more than one week, before their armies would be exhausted to the point where they would de-escalate, and pull back fully, to recover, and again after several months clash again in the same poor Koma.

Their constant wars were so often, that male people in those kingdoms were born only as war machines to be fed to the Koma. Rulers in both Kingdoms were older women with at least 60 centuries. Boys never made it to the first century unless they were working as baby machines or historians.

Their wars in Koma, with their huge and ever-expanding armies, being killed in massive numbers created a hill, that would enlarge as a new war was fought, and again and again.

Historians in both kingdoms taught different aspects of history and differed in their explanations, which would be the reason why they always fought.

Rima had a very fertile land and grew a special kind of plant that would provide all the energy and nutrients that their body needed for at least five days per single fruit. Those fruits had a very bad and terrible taste, which made Rima people hate them, but they had to take them to gain the profits associated with their energy and nutrients (as taking medication is for today's people). Ruma had nothing at all but a very arid climate which grew some hard structures and little stone-like tasty seeds that gave them energy for only several hours, Ruma would later use those hard structures in their wars against Rima as weapons.

The war was fought in such a balanced manner that for all the dozen millennials of fighting, there was no visible change on the borderline in Koma. It followed a simple logic which turns out to be that the Rima people had more energy to fight derived from their fruits, and the Ruma people had formidable weapons which had some advantage as the energy fruits. As soon as the Rima people were to lose, the Ruma people would lose energy and give Rima the upper hand, but it would have been too late that they would end in a stalemate all time.

Legends of Rima said that in Ruma they had those energetic plants that were sweeter, and legends of Ruma said that in Rima, they had bigger and softer tasty seeds. None of them was correct, but, the correct thing is that their wars were bloody, and based on the fact that people from the South wanted what people from the North couldn't give, and because people from the North wanted what the people from the South couldn't give too. As the two sides didn't communicate with each other, the situation worsened, so, their wars went on and on with no end in sight until one time.

One day, after days of intense preparations, one Rima youngster aged 0.7 century called Gararani and many of his other fellows, were ready to go to war with the Ruma people, but before he could march to the frontline, he talked with an unknown historian, that we won't know of, or what they talked about.

The story goes, as Gararani instead of taking that one fruit that everybody took, Gararani took one more fruit with him, dragging it in a sack, disguising it as a Rima weapon. Then the battle started, and there came the Ruma warriors, Rima took the beating of that time, some started to die, and then Ruma's energy degraded, hence the Rima turned the tide against them. They push and push and push, and again, it's a stalemate. The Koma was a sacred place to all two sides, as there were no burials, and everyone who died fighting would be found nowhere else apart from Koma, as the people who returned were only healthy people. In the time of counting the Rima warriors who were left, our Youngster Gararani was nowhere to be found, so his soul was tied to the Koma shrine.

For the people in Ruma, they always ended the battle with little energy, and their return was another part of the battle. When they were returning step by step, they would throw their remaining tools in secret places and remain only with a few hard tasty seeds that they would cut, and chew many times to gain additional energy that would push them home.

Our guy Gararani was in a pile of many victims of that endless war until he took a bite of that medicinal terrible fruit that he gained strength. As soon as he removed the bodies above him, he started to walk immediately, to see if he could catch up with the people in front of him. Till then, he didn't know whether he was going to Rima or Ruma, but he kept walking faster and faster, as he was powered by energetic fruit. It was not long until he realized that he was in Ruma, instead of Rima. With nowhere to go, he went on to that uncharted place with all possibilities in mind.

Then, he started to hear recessing footsteps and thought that he could follow them. With so much energy, he went closer and closer to Ruma warriors until he was a few shadows from them. Now that he was close enough, he waited to hear what they could say, but couldn't hear anything, which made him go closer to them until he joined them finally. To his surprise, the Ruma people didn't say anything and acted like nothing had happened yet, for him to discover later that the Ruma people didn't speak at all.

This story is too good and too long, and I am too tired to say it (so much fiction in this non-fiction book). I will write a book about it later, but let's get to the point and make a summary of later events, maybe if you are lucky enough you will get my second book.

The story goes like this, Gararani later leads those Ruma people to Rima, where they bring their sweet hard seeds that they chew, and Rima people in turn give their energetic fruits to the Ruma people. They both got energy and sweetness in sharing what they all got for their mutual benefit.

This Ruma-Rima story happens to us every time, where we can have some valuable item or service that we don't value, that other people value, and vice versa.

Okay, we are back to non-fiction. Everybody needs money, I want it, you want it, and they want it too. But there is magic in there! I don't want those useless papers, I want value associated with them, and that's why some currencies are more valuable than others. It is because we need money value and not those papers.

Think about it. If you give a certain service for money, or if you sell some product for money, the final step is that you will use that money to get service or buy a certain product, and hence, returning to where we started.
Now if you hadn't guessed it, there is a loophole there.
As far as I can tell, money is here to stay, and I am speaking about anything that can be used as a monetary medium. That thing will always stay.

When I speak I always throw many pieces and put them together later to make a point which I want to make, and I am going to do that briefly.

You see, everybody, wants money, but how we get that money that everyone wants is what makes us different. Some people can choose to provide services, while others can choose to give certain products. Again whether you like it or not, everyone who interacts with you needs something from you! That thing can be a solid physical thing such as a product, say a basket, or any non-physical random thing such as care.

Those things that they want from you, can be given for free, even though they can be sold too. And there is not even a thin margin between what can be sold and what can be given for free.

For some of us, in our childhood, we used to ask our parents for nearly everything we wanted, and if we were lucky and they were capable enough, they would satisfy our needs, free-of-charge. Need a song, you got it, clothes, there they are, ride, come on, and about rent, don't stress yourself, it has been taken care of.

And there comes adulthood, where you need to hustle hard, because all things you were being provided for free, now are costly as hell. Everything you need is to be paid for, and I am not sure if you can get all the money you want to get all the things you want.

This is the main reason why people join certain careers. But people did struggle too much and they still struggle and will struggle in the future. And for your information, there is no shortcut, we all have to pass in this phase. However, how we pass in this phase is what defines us for the rest of our lives, for the worse or better.

You want to live a simple, happy, and fancy life, but how can you live like that without money? – I don't know. That's where temptations come, can you lie, can you steal, can you put your morals down and the list of what you can offer goes on and on. You know about girls who started to look for wealthier men asking them for everything, ranging from shoes to iPhones, to cars, to houses? – That may be the reason, and this goes for the boys who want the same from rich women.

It is so strange that we all pass through this before making it in life, but even gold is melted in its refineries, so passing through a terrible time is not bad at all if it is not the end.

But, how can we pass this process intact? That's the problem, I always asked myself, and I am sure many people asked themselves the same question.

Is it too hard for you to transition from a life of dependence to life of independence? What if I told you that you can change that right away? And I am not a prophet, and this is not a kind of miracle, but it will certainly work for you.

We associate with people who have what we need, and we are associated with people who need something from us. And this is where the magic must happen- in between.

For me, I was a nice guy for most of my life, maybe I am still one, but it's other people who tell you so, and not yourself. So, people who were more knowledgeable than me, always told me that being a nice guy would drag me down, and for quite some time I thought they were correct, as being a nice guy was so exhausting for me.

Do you remember about the loophole I mentioned in the first chapter? Well if not, it is about how money is used to buy services or products, and then the sellers use that same money to buy other services or products, and the circle goes on and on, that is the very foundation of the monetary system- that is Monetary circulation.

So in my life as a nice guy, I would create and take part in glitches of the matrix in a way that I didn't know at the time!
I know you are wondering how, but it is so simple.
I would do something for free, as long as I considered the recipient as a friend (they always come to your rescue when you are to provide them with something that would

require money if done by strangers). But later, I would discover that people whom I helped with my skills for free, would go on to provide them for money, and they would make huge amounts of money, while I was left in the dust.

Well, then I knew that being a nice guy is so exhausting, but it's who I am, and I couldn't change it, I knew somehow that in one way or another, I could use that character to be profitable to me too.

For example, it was not long ago that I offered free video-making services, that I realized that you can't make money, merely from giving free things, counting on unknown possible clients, that you don't know about, hence as Post Malone says, Waiting for Never.

That's when I came up with the idea of how I could give services for free to get money!
You heard me well, the loophole follows a simple logic that there is no free service at all, it depends on who gives it to you, how they give it to you, and why they give it to you. Say, for example, Financial advice (I had to come up with a neutral and inoffensive word, but you can come up with any example). Some people pay huge sums of money to get it, and sometimes other people get it for free.

The wisdom remains only in knowing when to provide that free service, who you are going to provide it to when you are going to provide it, and for how long. It's not a miracle and anyone can take part in this system and later see the real magic happening.

For starters, it goes as if you would give a certain service for free, let's say the financial advice example from above, and then after the first, or second time giving that service free of charge (given you have built trust and profitability for the other party - receiver), the next time, if you charge him a reasonable amount of money, he/she will not hesitate to give you that whole sum of money.

But you have to be very careful about everything in the process. You have to make sure that the other party doesn't get the full grasp of what you are up to. And the importance of this is that they will gain the profits consciously and pay you back unconsciously.

The good thing is that I didn't spoil your amazement or your plan because even I would not be aware of this effect if it was done to me! (I don't know about you, but results are nearly the same – if done correctly, you won't notice what's happening until it's done)

It is the same driving force that Marketing and Psychology carry with them too, and that is Perception. They don't reveal what they are up to until they get it. This is the same tactic that we will use in our ways too.

Have you ever seen a Disk Jockey at a certain party who plays good songs, and after say 10 songs is given a huge sum of money as a tip as he made people happy? The DJ is paid by the event organizers to play songs, but he/she receives the tip as a bonus. It is the same situation as a waiter or waitress whose responsibility is to serve the clients, but they can also be given tips depending on the satisfaction of their clients and their wealth.

The place for the perception in the human mind is so great, that we value certain things that we must not value and give less value to valuable things.

See for example, a person can give Five hundred Rwandan francs to a DJ as a tip, but the same person can't give a starving child on the road, even one thousand Rwandan francs.

I am not here for a moral lesson about what's right and what's wrong, but I am sure that the driving force in these two activities is perception, and has nothing to do with morals (from my point of view).

In order to define how it works, let's look back at the point I made in the first chapter! We need money to do many things, and of course among them is happiness. So, believe it or not, when someone makes you happy, you are tempted to give him/her money, because it is why you need money – to buy happiness. Again in our DJ example, when the DJ plays the song, it is perceived by the audience as if he/she is providing them with free service, then, whenever he creates a dopamine spike in his/her wealthy audience, they can base their judgment on their perception and give huge sum of money to that DJ.

Now it is time to match the dots. The free services provision scheme that I want to highlight, works on the same principle that a certain DJ, or Waiter/Waitress uses to receive massive tips.

If you provide a certain free service, given other factors are favorable (right person, right time, right service, and right frequency), the other party at the receiving end perceives that service as its benefit, and bases its happiness and satisfaction on it. So, when the recipient gets that free service for the first time, He/she is excited. Give that service again free of charge, and the recipient will be more than grateful that will create that dopamine spike that a DJ gives when he plays the best songs for his audience. And you know what's next? The recipient will give the service provider the amount of money that He/she thinks is as valuable as the two services that He/she has been provided with. But that recipient will do that unconsciously and He/she will perceive the action in favor of his/her side, in terms of profitability.

The good thing about this perception is that the two sides are all satisfied! The service provider gets the unexpected sum of money, which He/she never thought about (in case of how much, or when he/she would get it). The recipient is grateful for the kindness and generosity of the service provider, which results in the pay of nearly equal value worth of fortune, again, it's a win-win situation.

I hope that nobody was caught up in the process of changing perspective, as I wrote this book from the Service provider's point of view. Given the situation of the free-service provision that comes with perception to the recipient, there are several profits in the process that I would like to talk about.

I am not going to talk about the recipient side but on the service provision side. In case you missed it, all the two sides are in the win-win situation, so profits are made on both sides. But the point I want to make is that the service provider side is what uses this free-service method to make money, hence, the side that I want to emphasize too much on.

There are many profits made on the service provider side that anyone can come with. For me, the most important are three, and I am going to speak about them in a random order.

The first targeted profit and the reason for this whole trick is the monetary profit. Think about it, you are providing a payable service, and you want that pay so bad but you are so good that you want to perceive the receiver that it is a free service. Luckily, in all circumstances, that service carries with it the monetary value that both sides know, at least consciously.

So, when you provide a certain service for free, believe me, if you did it in the right way, it is worth the same monetary value. Then, you provide that service for free again, and the monetary value it carries with it sums up together to make a reasonable price, that the recipient can give unconsciously. The point here is, that you don't have to worry, if you can provide a certain service for free, as in some way or another, that price will resurface again and make it, in the final calculations.

Here, someone can think that the price associated with the given service reduces over time, and I think that they are correct, counting on inflation, but the good thing is that the value will always be there if other factors are right! (I will talk about this in the last chapter). Have you provided a costly service for free, and then in return been provided with a costly service free of charge too? That's what I am talking about! These services are still valuable in terms of monetary cost, but when they are provided for free, that cost doesn't vanish, instead, it is transferred to other valuable forms, such as being provided with nearly equal value service or being given an equal monetary value in form of unconscious gifts.

The second profit associated with the provision of valuable services free of charge is the Friendship between the two parties and the privileges that come with it.
From my experience, it was easier to give a friend of mine a certain service for me, even if it was costly if provided by a stranger. But friends are friends, and they may reach a point where they can omit the need for money in their exchanges. Even though this method can work on friends

to some extent, it is not what I am talking about. The reason for this is that friends meet for many different reasons, and the profitability of their relations can vary.

What I want to say, is that you don't have to wait for friends to take the first step to come to you to ask for a given service! Instead, you will have to take the first step and choose people that you want to associate with, in a way that you could make noticeable gains.

In this way, you can provide them with a service free of charge, and do it a couple of times, until they start to think of you as a caring and generous person. Diverting from the first point, the second point of friendship is much long-lasting and if extracted in the best way can bring many privileges that contribute to the overall growth of an individual.

Many people overlook the importance of friendship in the moneymaking process, but it is as valuable as the money itself (maybe).

For me, I used, and still use friendship in my money-spending schemes, and it can work in the moneymaking processes too. How it worked is that I could befriend a certain seller in a way that he/she could consider me as a friend.
Starting was always the hardest part, as I would sacrifice a huge amount of money as required by the seller on the first run! I would come the next time and bargain to reduce the price of the service or the product and voila, it's done!

The following time, I would come and use my previous bargaining power, while mixing it with the fact that I am a premium customer and bring up the highest price that he/she sold to me for the first time when I went there. The result would always be that the seller would start to decrease the price below the normal selling price by taking into account the friendship that I had with him/her. The best part is that from that point going forward, the price would be fixed at that minimum amount considering that the seller got at least a threshold profit.

The benefit of this friendship unlike old-fashioned friendships, is that there is mutual respect between two people in focus. It is because, you met in a respectful manner, which is business, and he/she owes you respect as a premium client.

This being said, it is important to note that the free service provision also falls in the same category as the example above, where friendship can be of the utmost value. In most cases, because this friendship is in a professional way, it would result in the service provider hiring them, or working with them in more future projects.

The reason why I brought this up, is because most of the time you get more like the friends whom you associate with. If you are associated with people who drink alcohol, it is more likely that you will try alcohol too, and if you are associated with non-alcoholic people, you are more likely to reduce the amount of alcohol you take in. The same goes for religious people, toxic people, or sports people.

Now, ask yourself what can happen if you are associated with rich people as your friends. It is more likely that you will become rich too if you play it right. Remember, friends choose you because they want something from you. You are not going to throw them away, but you need to choose other friends that you can get something from! If it is money that you want, you are going to choose rich people. If it is ideas that you want, you are going to choose intelligent people and associate with them, and you will do this for everything that you will need, and so on, and so on.

Let's say you have a million-dollar project but you are stuck with poor friends (only if it is because of their poor mindset) that project will never be put into practice, and it is more likely to die in the thinker's brain, without seeing the light of day.

Contrary, if you are to associate with rich friends, say thousand-dollar friends, you are more likely to come up with much better ideas and create more realistic approaches to your projects, based either on your friend's ideas or experience. (If they are not toxic or jealous). In simple words, you are more likely to think and act like your friends (people who you associate with) which makes this point of friendship more useful.

The third profit associated with the free-of-charge service provision is the experience and professionalism that you get while providing that certain service. Think about it, you are doing something that has the potential to give you money, but you get better every time you do it. The process ensures that you get exposure to how the moneymaking system works while excelling at what you do and near your future customers.

I saw this firsthand, as every new video I made kept getting better and better, also the process was getting easier, as I got used to the work very much. It is the same as getting a free internship.

It is too hard to be hired by a given company or individual if you are to compete with other experienced individuals. When you provide them with a free service, you get out from the crowd and distinguish yourself from others. Until then, there is no need for heated competition, as you are working as a respectful friend. As you improve at what you are doing, the recipient will have the realization that there is no need for competition, and you will win that job in that way.

The importance of this is that you are not going to beg to get a job, instead, you are going to provide something and get a job on favorable terms. Some workers already know the importance of this concept, and when they are going to be hired, they turn the tables in their favor and show the Hiring bodies, that they don't want the job to be successful, instead that the Hiring body needs them to be successful.

To make these points more understandable, let's put all of them together. You try to give a service for free, but the recipient side can decide (is more likely) to pay back for the given service the amount of money that equals the given service. In the process of the service provision, the provider wins the trust and is befriended by the recipient to the extent that their relationship can bring more profits. A last point I emphasized, is the knowledge development of the service provider, who gets firsthand information of how the moneymaking process works and can be hired in the way.

There are great profits in the free service provision, and as you have seen, free services aren't free at all if the play is right. Okay, the best way to move to the next chapter

For some, you may have provided a free service in your life, or you would like to give it a try. I am not going to stop you right away, but free services come at a cost, and that's what I am going to talk about in this chapter.

Have you ever thought about the fact that construction workers in the same city are nearly on the same level of knowledge/skills? But yet they provide a wide range of buildings! Amazingly, a mason who builds a fence knows nearly as much as a mason who erects a skyscraper or builds an amazing bridge. It is also important to know that as their work varies greatly, their wages also vary.

The reason for their wage imbalance is to be attributed mainly to the people whom they work for. This is correct for many areas and fields too. This is to say that irrespective of the same level of knowledge, you may be paid less or more wage than other people in consideration because you work for different people/organizations.

To put this in our free-service provision scheme, one must know that what some people care about, other people care less, and what you think is useless may turn out to be of impressive value to the right receivers.

There is a wide range of services that you can try to see if this free-service provision works. But don't rush yourself, Rome wasn't built overnight!

Think about nearly every impressive thing, and you will find that it started as a joke somewhere in the past. Take an example of an impressive human work such as a spaceship. It is hard to think that it evolved from a simple thing such as a stone! No need to turn this into a history lesson, but spaceships evolved from fighting projectiles. Wars were fought using stones, eventually turning to arrows, then to canons, and later to rockets. It was the rivalry between the US and Nazi Germany that saw the evolutionary V2 rockets, which were later modified to serve the specific purpose of sending payloads in the Orbit. And here we are, spaceships bigger than anyone can imagine, but from the simplest object as stone.

This is why nobody should overlook the importance of progress even if it can be at a slow pace.

In our primary focus of a free-service provision, there are many aspects that the provider must take into account before providing that service.

First, one should know that the receiving side really wants what the provider is offering. Otherwise, it is a yin and yang difference, and your service will pass like a weekend holiday. This point is very disturbing since no one knows what the other person is thinking, and everyone must be aware of that and avoid it in every possible way.

As advice to the varying personal preferences. It is better to stick to generalization practice and put yourself on the receiver's end. This can omit the prolonged period of knowing his/her personal preferences, but will also reduce the personal impact that the service will have on his/her conscious persona. If it is shortsighted profit, you can use generalization and deliver your free service that will scratch his/her heart lightly. But if you are more of a long-sighted person, you have to study the receiver carefully, and closely by simulating and stimulating certain interactions, to see how he/she reacts to these different interactions. It is after concluding that one can take action and boom, everything plays out.

After knowing that the receiver's end needs a certain service that is within your abilities, the second thing you must see is if you have competitors who provide the same service. There may be a couple of competitors or potential competitors, but it is not your problem, instead theirs, as you will not demand money! – Yes it's a free service. But again, even if I need shoes, I can't take old people's shoes because they are free, passing on reasonably priced shoes that fit me well. You need to have at least a minimum quality of service that you are going to provide, even if it is free. If it is not good at all, you need to sit down and work on it, instead of going around and offering it everywhere as bad luck.

If your service is good, at least on a bearable level or the same level as your competitors, make the first approach, and you will obscure the receiver from seeing your competitors. Now, it is too risky if your competitors know this trick and utilize it the same way you used it, the reason why you must maximize your output, even if it is for free.

The third thing you must take into account when offering free service is the financial status of the receiver. In the previous chapter, the focus on being friends with the receiver assumed that the receiver has a higher financial status than the receiver, and that is the best scenario of what can happen. In case it goes wrong with calculating the financial status of the receiver, it is better to move on and consider that service as a free service! – Yes, it was still a free service, but consider it more like a friendly free service and move on. Even if you can see that you miscalculated before the fact, first deliver your service and move on thereafter. The good thing is that it is still profitable with the said profits in the previous chapter omitting money, and that's too good reason to be extracted.

The last but not the least aspect you must take into account when providing a certain service for free is the overall cost of the service on your side. It is said that you must hope for the best, but prepare for the worst, and that's what we are going to do. First thing first, you need to make sure that whether the service is free or not can't change your financial stability much. Business is business, and you need to take care of yourself before you start to worry about others. So if the service that you will provide for free will jeopardize your financial well-being, go away from it.

Other aspects will be met as you progress through your work, and you will need to utilize multiple methods to divert from bad occasions on the road to prosperity.

I am done for this chapter, and there's nothing else I can say apart from GOODLUCK.

The method highlighted in this book is a simulation of real-life activities. But what if this method doesn't work for you at all? Well, the problem isn't the method said or yourself. The problem is in between, in the implementation of the free service provision.

In this book, I was careful enough to highlight that only services can be provided for free. It is not because products can not be provided for free, but it's another topic and requires additional protocols. In short, because products have production costs amounting to much of the price of the product, were the product to be given for free, the production cost would be much higher than the income, and the institution involved in that practice would fall into bankruptcy. The case is left only for huge industrial complexes that can absorb the shock of product vanishing without relying on insurance companies. If you are not in a big industrial complex, it is better to remain with paid product provision or partial discounts which would help your business to remain afloat.

For the case of inefficient exploitation of the triple profits said herein, one must assess these profits individually and draw a conclusion based on them, whether he/she can continue to provide that service for free or abandon it altogether.

One can say for example, that he made money, but he/she did not stay as a respectful friend of the service receiver. The only reason for this can be the poor communication between the two sides, or misconduct and bad behavior of either side. Although the importance of these two characteristics varies from place to place, they remain as the core pillars for prosperity in service provision. It is impossible to remain in the service provision service while having poor communication skills or terrible behavior, at least only if you provide free services, and they will accept it only for a brief period. Another possibility would be if the individual has an exceptional talent-knowledge-skills set which would make him/her impossible to replace and that situation would be temporary, as there would be an indefinite search for his/her replacement. Have miscommunication or misconduct originates from the receiver's side, as the free service provider, you must break the bond as soon as possible and part ways.

Misconduct and miscommunication can come in many ways, but the prominent form is if either side doesn't respect the other. In case of this behavior, it is important to stay calm and look for other options instead of forcing things. Remember that you need to protect your reputation.

Lastly, you may choose to provide a certain service for free, with no production cost spent and no visible change to the receiving end. This is the common form of free service provision and one must calculate it in the form of monetary form to guess the amount of prestige that he/she would get back from the receiver. It is easy to correlate the amount of monetary value a certain service carries with it to estimate what the payback may be. From these estimations, one can see that services that carry some or no monetary value at all receive small or no payback.

To solve such paradox, one must master a certain service that carries with it high monetary value to receive bigger paychecks. This works as payable services and one must maximize the quality of the service that he/she is providing. It can be done by learning a new skill that can sell itself.

It is also necessary to note that not all services can be provided for free, but most can.

I think now is the time to draw a conclusion, where I can say that free services aren't free at all.
One must master the process of free-service provision before engaging in it and take everything into account to reach the greater good.

I tried to answer the reason why someone can pass on a beggar and give him one coin or two, and spend several hundred dollars on a DJ or a Pastor.

The method highlighted in this book can be/is being used by individuals, companies, countries, or even bigger organizations.